# How to Bond with Your Child Through Books

*One Family's Plan to Read 100 Books Together*

*(With Bonus 5-Year Update)*

Galynne Howard Matichuk

To my most amazing children, N!ck and GrAce,

When I look back over the years of your childhood, one of my most favorite memories will be reading together.

We've read many amazing and wonderful stories. Now it is your turn to go forth and write your own.

# CONTENTS

# ACKNOWLEDGMENTS

There are several people who deserve our thanks.

Long before we ever took the first step on our journey to one hundred books, my parents pointed me in the right direction. My mother-in-law came alongside at a critical moment and changed the direction of our path. My sister made the travel through books so much more enjoyable. My sister-in-law brought inspiration and encouragement. Their steps made it possible for us to take our steps.

Thanks to my parents for surrounding my sister and me with books and for showing us what it looks like to be a reader.

Thanks to my father, Tom, for reading to my sister and me when we were young. My two favorites? *Green Eggs and Ham* by Dr. Seuss, and *The Lion, the Witch and The Wardrobe* by C. S. Lewis. I've never forgotten, and I could listen to you forever. Thank you most of all for the example, inspiration and legacy you set by starting and ending every day with reading your Bible. I was watching. My children are watching now.

Thanks to my mother, Grace, who took my sister and me regularly to the library and allowed us to spend hours lost in the pages of a good book. Thanks for reading to us when we were children. I especially remember snuggling in your bed, propped up with pillows, as you read to us. Thank you for being a practical cheerleader extraordinaire. (Don't worry. I'll find a way to get the tape residue off my cabinets.)

Thanks to my sister, Leanne, who often rubbed backs while I read. The kids loved it, and it added a unique touch to our reading – figuratively and literally! Thank you for all the nighttime reading that you've done as well, although I find it suspicious that you lose the ability to tell time when you're in charge of putting the kids to bed. The kids thank you for their extended hours and their backrubs. They can never get enough.

Thanks to my mother-in-law, Eileen, for finding *Roar!*. It changed the course of our reading. Thanks for all the times, and there have been many, when you have encouraged me to write.

Thanks to my sister-in-law, Allison, for showing me your Kindle book, *How to Write an Opinion Essay: A Foolproof Guide to the Basics*. I thought that it was practical, creative and well-written. I love that you began with the simple goal of helping your niece and son write a paper, and your efforts have grown into a book that will help many others. Thank you as well for your example, which inspired me to write a Kindle book of my own. Thank you most of all for your friendship, my Sister-Friend.

Thank you to my husband, Chris, for all the support, encouragement, fun stories, and your inspired idea to read through the Bible as a family. Thanks as well for doing all the driving so I could read.

Thank you to my wonderful children, N!ck and GrAce. If I could choose any two children in the world, I would choose you. I am so proud of you – the way you think, process, engage, analyze and share. You're brilliant. You're creative. You amaze me. I thank God for you every day.

Thank you to everyone. I am forever grateful.

# 1 THE GOAL

Several years ago, our family set a goal to read one hundred books aloud together.

To be honest, I set the goal and dragged everyone along. But I didn't have to drag them far. After only a few novels, the power of good literature took over and my kids begged me to read whenever possible. Adding in candy rewards helped too!

This is the story of our journey which, to be even more honest, didn't begin with one hundred books. It began with one and grew from there.

We hope you find our story interesting, informative and inspirational. More importantly, we hope you consider embarking on a similar adventure with your family.

But why would your family want to read one book together, let alone one hundred?

Because it's about more than books.

Our decision to read one hundred books together created an opportunity to share, discover, and build into each other, strengthening our bonds as a family.

I believe that when my kids are grown and look back on their childhood, one of their best and happiest memories will have been reading together. And it will be one of my favorite memories as well.

Here's how it happened...

## 2  THE FIRST STEP

Every journey begins with a destination in mind, and my goal was simple.

I wanted my children to be readers. More specifically, I wanted them to love reading the way that I did when I was a child, and still do as an adult.

No one had to ask me to read when I was younger. I devoured books. I spent many happy hours curled up on the corner of our couch, a crisp red apple in one hand and a good novel in the other. I'm sure I wore a permanent spot in the cushion.

When I had children of my own, I wanted them to share my love of books. From their earliest years, I tried various strategies to introduce my son and daughter to literature. My husband and I read short stories to them before bedtime. We watched television programs like 'Between the Lions' and 'Reading Rainbow' that promoted reading. We went regularly to the library, participating in the free programs.

My children seemed to enjoy all of these activities. But they weren't becoming avid readers, as I had hoped.

My son, who turned nine years old and was in the Fourth Grade, was reluctant. I had to insist that he read. Even then, he just flipped through the same books over and over again.

My daughter, who turned seven years old and was in Second Grade, was fast and sloppy. She skipped over words she didn't know, and often missed huge concepts in the plot.

My husband didn't set a great example himself. He had always struggled with reading and rarely picked up a book unless it was related to work and had more computer code than text.

So I felt discouraged, and a bit fearful.

I knew the academic importance of reading. Success in school depends upon being able to gather, understand, analyze and apply information gained through printed material.

I knew the personal importance of reading. When we finish a good book, we walk away enriched with information, inspiration, wonder, discovery, empathy, and a new experience or perspective. We are changed by what we read.

I was determined to find a way to get my kids to fall in love with reading.

As I continued to search for something to spark their interest, I remembered one of my all-time favorite books - *The Lion, the Witch and the Wardrobe* by C. S. Lewis, the second in a seven-book series called The Chronicles of Narnia.

The kids were advanced enough to read it. Surely this story would capture their hearts if they gave it a chance. But I suspected my son would skim through the pages and felt confident my daughter would do the same.

So, I came up with a solution. I would read the book out loud to them. Then, I could emphasize the clever charm, check for comprehension, point out the subtle humor, and explain the spiritual lessons.

Without realizing it, that decision became our first step on a path that would lead us far beyond a single novel.

# 3 THE JOURNEY BEGINS

We had a goal. Read one book aloud as a family. We had a strategy. Read together at bedtime.

Then something happened that completely transformed everything. I told my mother-in-law what we were doing.

My mother-in-law liked what she heard, and hoped that others in the family might do the same thing. At Christmas that year, she ordered a book called *Roar! A Christian Family Guide to the Chronicles of Narnia* by Heather Kopp with David Kopp. She had intended to give it to someone else, but that person didn't want it. So my mother-in-law offered it to anyone who was interested, and I pounced on it.

The book *Roar!* (title shortened for simplicity) is a chapter-by-chapter guide to all seven books in The Chronicles of Narnia. Each entry includes a short chapter summary, adult analysis, questions, and other fun features such as British translations, fascinating facts and activities to try at home. The guide also has a detailed section on the author, C. S. Lewis, and two 'final exams', one easy and one more challenging.

Suddenly, simply reading *The Lion, The Witch and the Wardrobe* wasn't enough. Thanks to our new resource book, our family could dive deep and work through the novel. And we didn't have to stop there. We could read the whole series, and when we finished, we'd take the final exams. I would even offer a prize for the highest score.

I informed my husband and children of the new and ambitious plan to read all seven books, and everyone seemed pleased with the idea. Bedtime reading wouldn't be enough, so we came up with two additional times that worked best for our family. We could work through the novels during evening meals, and when driving together. Thankfully, I'm one of those fortunate individuals who doesn't get car sick when I read in a moving vehicle.

And so we began. I remember the first evening that we gathered around the table and enjoyed supper while I read. At the end of the first chapter, I asked the questions from *Roar!*. Everyone was engaged, and my husband even shared a story from his childhood that we'd never heard before. I couldn't have been more pleased. We were off to a fabulous start, and I was certain we'd sail blissfully through the rest of the book.

How naïve of me.

# 4 LESSON FROM AN ALLIGATOR

It didn't take long for the excitement to fade. Three chapters, to be exact. The kids still enjoyed listening to the story, but yawned when I asked questions and gave half-hearted answers or none at all.

This was bad. It could spell early disaster. But then I remembered something I'd been told about alligators, and that information saved our reading.

I have had several opportunities to tour Gatorland in Florida, first as a child and later as an adult. One visit might have been enough for most people, but I have a grudging fascination with those green, scaly reptiles. They're ugly, fairly dumb, deceptively lazy, yet frightfully lethal. The combination makes them cool, in a horrifying way.

During my second visit to Gatorland, I happened to strike up a conversation with one of the workers, and we chatted for over an hour. Among other things, he talked about training the gators to do simple tricks. I hadn't thought this was possible, considering their small brains. But the worker explained that anything can be trained with food. I never forgot that line. And if dumb gators could be motivated with treats, so could reluctant kids.

The fourth evening of reading went as expected. My children listened to the chapter, then offered lame answers to the questions. But this time, I was prepared. I put down the book, walked over to our pantry, and pulled out a bin of 'healthy' candy. Well, it was as healthy as candy could get. No artificial colors, dyes, flavors, preservatives, sweeteners or hydrogenated oils. But it was still candy, and that's why it worked.

I placed the container, filled with jelly beans and gummy fruit slices, in the middle of the table. Then, I set out the rules. One candy for a good answer. Two candies for a really good answer.

It was as if a surge of energy shot through the room. Suddenly my kids, who don't get a lot of sweet treats, were fighting to answer first, or add extra details to someone else's response. It was beautiful, and I loved every minute of it.

My husband even got in on the action, although I must admit that he didn't earn many candies, at least not in the beginning.

This was great! The bowl of candy became a fixed feature as we worked our way through chapter after chapter. The family continued to listen attentively and eagerly offered solid answers to each question, hands outstretched to receive their treats. It was everything for which I had hoped.

But I was wrong to expect so little. There was so much more.

## 5  A GLIMPSE OF MORE

It began as a typical evening supper. We had just finished chapter eight from *The Voyage of the Dawn Treader*, the 5th book in The Chronicles of Narnia. I pulled out the bin of candy, and read a seemingly simple question from our guide book, *Roar!*.

*"Have you ever dreamed of finding buried treasure or suddenly becoming very rich? Would having a lot of money change how you behave or treat other people? (Be honest!)" p 203*

My son said that being rich wouldn't change him. Then he hesitated, looked down, and said that if he had more money, maybe kids at school would treat him better.

That was not what I expected to hear. Suddenly, I needed to hear more. After several follow-up questions, we learned that my son was being bullied by three boys in his class.

In that moment, several feelings washed over me. Shock. Protective mother bear anger. And an overwhelming gratitude that we had read together that night. I don't know how long it would have taken, how bad it would have gotten, or how I would have found out otherwise.

We put down the book, discussed the situation, and came up with strategies for how my son could handle himself at school. At the first opportunity, I informed the teacher about what was happening, and her careful and brilliant mediation brought about a positive resolution with an end to the bullying.

Later on, I wondered about the wording of the question, and the specific advice to 'be honest'. I was curious to see if that phrase had been used with any other questions. I flipped through the entire book, and that is the only time I could find those exact directions. Did those words give my son the courage that he needed? I don't know. But I'm so glad that he listened and answered the question honestly.

That experience shifted something for me. My focus changed. It got bigger.

I still wanted my kids to read more and read better. I still hoped they would become avid, life-long readers. But more than anything, I wanted to have more moments like the one we'd just had. I wanted to seize the opportunity to build into our family and have meaningful discussions together that we would never forget.

My vision got bigger as well. I didn't want to stop reading after one book. Or even seven. I wanted to keep the conversations going.

So once we finished the seven books in the The Chronicles of Narnia, I proposed the outrageous goal of reading 100 books aloud together as a family. Great novels and more candy? I didn't have to twist any arms.

We had no idea how long it would take, which books we would choose, or even if we could do it. But we were on our way.

# 6  THE POWER OF CANDY

Candy has played an absolutely crucial role in our reading. I confess that the treats started as a bribe to motivate better participation. But as with so many other things, the sweet rewards have become much more.

I should probably cough up another confession. Although I began with the purest organic candy possible, I have allowed my standards to slip. In the interest of variety and continued motivation, I added cheap and inferior candy to our stash. We also used other substitutes such as bags of potato chips, sprinkle-covered donuts, or ice cream treats. Ah, I feel better after that disclosure. No one's perfect, and I can live with any nutritional guilt because I'm so pleased with the results.

When we first began reading, I carried two items with me - our current book and a bowl full of candy. It didn't matter whether we were at the table, in the car or tucked into bed, I had that container of sweets. Whenever one of my kids or my husband gave a good answer, they immediately chose a candy.

We did establish two rules. First, if we were eating supper, the candy had to be placed off to the side until the meal was finished. Second, if we were reading at night, the kids had to brush their teeth after any consumption of sugar.

I'm sure it's no surprise that the kids wanted to earn as much candy as possible. Typically, they walked away from a reading session with about six to eight small treats. Eight jelly beans wasn't a huge amount, that's for sure. But it felt like more when their sibling or father only got five treats. It wasn't long before the amount of candy stopped being the main goal. What really counted was earning more candy than anyone else.

The competition was intense. Instead of gobbling down each candy as they earned it, the kids began lining up their treats in plain sight. That made it very evident who had answered the most questions or responded with greater detail or insight . . . and gave them the opportunity to rub it in.

Not only did the kids want to beat each other, but they also wanted to top their father. This wasn't so hard in the beginning, but things have changed. My husband has changed. He has become an insightful force to reckon with, and he's more than happy to point out whenever he beats the kids to an answer or earns more treats. He's also the best at rubbing it in.

Did this competition and light mockery bother me? Not at all. I loved it. The answers kept getting better and better.

In another surprising turn, the competition became so intense that the kids were no longer willing to wait for me to ask questions. They began offering unsolicited insights or comments, often followed by the one-word question, "Candy?"

Was this growing beyond my original intentions? Yes, and I'm happy to admit it. In fact, any time has become a fair time to earn a coveted treat. It doesn't matter if we're watching a movie, hanging with friends, biking to the store, or talking about our day. If my kids can make a clever connection to a book we're reading or have read, that's worth a candy.

Again, this was beyond my expectations. I never would have thought that my children would be offering so many personal insights, competing to share ideas, and critically analyzing situations and characters, even when we weren't reading. It was amazing.

When it came to passing out the treats, I tried to strike a balance between *quality* and *quantity*. Candy could only be earned by intelligent, creative and insightful comments. That was the quality. But once the intelligence started to flow, so did the candy. That was the quantity.

Answers didn't always have to be correct. As long as a response could be reasonably defended, there was a reward. A plausible prediction, even if not right, earned a treat. Even laughing at the right time, showing comprehension and appreciation of the humor, earned a jelly bean or gummy bear.

There is a downside to our system, and I recognize the health concerns with too much sugar consumption. I also recognize that some individuals may suggest I'm turning my children into greedy gluttons who expect a reward for every clever comment. They would be partially correct, on both counts. I feel the benefits outweigh the risks. Besides, my children don't get much candy, outside of our reading, and the rewards for answers have become more like points earned during a fun game.

There has been an interesting twist over the last few years of our reading. As we expanded the places we read, I couldn't always carry the container of candy with me. So I traded the bowl for a pencil and a sheet of paper. The paper served as my new bookmark, but more importantly, I used it to record the candy earned by making tally marks on the sheet. Then, anyone could "purchase a candy" at a later date, and I simply crossed off the tally marks. This system has worked surprisingly well.

We've added an additional element to measure the 'degree of difficulty' of the questions and answers. For simple questions, the reward is one candy or one tally mark. For more difficult questions, it might be two or three candies or tally marks. But for a brilliant response, above and beyond what's expected, we yell "Big candy", and the 'answeree' earns five tally marks at once. That's a big reward to recognize a big answer.

Are we stretching the reward system? Perhaps, but it's a huge deal to earn a big candy, and everyone works hard for them.

We've also come up with different ways to cash in the candies. When we are near a candy store, we work out a loose formula of how many candies equals how many tally marks. Sometimes they'll cash in thirty tally marks for a whole chocolate bar, a bag of potato chips, or a bulk bag of mixed candy. As the kids have grown older and their desires have changed, I've allowed them to cash in the tally points for computer time or money.

As you can see, there's a lot of flexibility with the tally points. I want everyone to enjoy what they've earned. I also want them to continue being motivated to earn more.

As an added bonus, it's easy for anyone to join our reward system. When the grandparents stay with us for a few weeks, their names are added to our tally sheet and they earn candies like everyone else. It's surprising how competitive those grandparents can be! But what I love best is the wisdom and perspective they bring to the conversation.

As time has gone on, I've noticed that my kids have cashed in their tally points less often. They still fight to earn candy and compare who has the most. But it's become more of a status symbol or bragging right. And my husband is the one who brags the most.

An unforeseen bonus with the candy is that it allows me to give a lot of positive reinforcement.

As my kids approach their teen years, there seems to be more opportunities for conflict. We argue over keeping rooms clean, getting homework done, doing chores, spending too much time on the computer, and watching attitudes. But every time we pick up a book, there's a chance to compliment my teens, with words of affirmation and a sweet, tangible reward.

Perhaps most surprising and wonderful of all, 'candy' has become our special family code word.

When my kids say something clever or offer an insight, they ask, "Candy?"

It's more than a request for a treat. They're really asking, "What did you think? Do you like what I said? Did you think that was smart?"

When I reply, "Yes, candy", I'm saying much more.

I'm telling my kids, "Well done. That was clever. I'm proud of you. I enjoy hearing your thoughts. Tell me more."

Hearing that message has become more important than the treat, although they'll still take both.

So I apologize to doctors, dentists, nutritionists and others who feel we may be setting a bad example. I'm sorry...but the candy stays.

# 7 CHOOSING GREAT BOOKS

Our family sailed through the seven books in The Chronicles of Narnia. With a colorful bowl of candy (replenished often) and the excellent resource *Roar!* as our guide, it couldn't have been easier. However, once we finished the series, we ran into a snag.

How were we going to choose the next novel to read? And the other ninety-two after that?

We began with books that I knew well, my childhood favorites. These were titles like *Charlie and The Chocolate Factory* by Roald Dahl, *The Penderwicks* by Jeanne Birdsall, *The Best Christmas Pageant Ever* by Barbara Robinson, and *Where the Red Fern Grows* by Wilson Rawls.

I owned some of these books, borrowed others from the library, and bought a few of the classics, especially ones I hoped my kids would reread.

About the time I was running low on titles and starting to search through library guides and online lists, my son suggested that we read one of his favorite books, *Swindle*, by Gordon Korman.

At first, I wasn't sure this was a good idea. My original plan had been to introduce the family to new novels and authors. My son had already read *Swindle* several times. What value would there be for him to read it again? Besides, he'd know all the answers and wouldn't earn as many candies.

But the more I thought about it, the more I embraced the idea.

I'm the kind of person who goes to a restaurant and orders the same item every time, without fail. We used to frequent a local Thai restaurant and the owners knew me so well that they'd start making my order when I walked in the door.

Even though I always chose the mussamun chicken curry (with the lowest possible level of spice because of my wimpy palate), I never grew tired of it. In fact, I looked forward to ordering it again. There's something wonderful about the anticipation of a much-loved meal.

I realized it wasn't any different for my son. He really enjoyed *Swindle*. If he wanted to hear it again, why would I deny him that pleasure? The book wouldn't lose any of its quality by reading it aloud together, and my son might even gain new insights or catch something he'd missed.

As my son continued to lobby for his book, I realized how important it was for him to share a favorite book with his family. Hmmm . . . much like I wanted to share the books that I loved with them.

At that moment, I was struck by a humbling insight. This wasn't *my* list of books. It was *our* list of books. My kids were moving from being passive participants, to taking an active interest and ownership in our family activity.

So, I agreed wholeheartedly, and we laughed our way through Swindle, which is a great story. Each time a new book in the series came out, we were among the first to buy it. Our family has so enjoyed Gordon Korman as an author that 23 of the books we've read were penned by him.

I did have to work extra hard to come up with questions for my son, since he was already familiar with the plot. Perhaps he didn't get quite as many candies, but he didn't mind missing out. I think he liked the power of knowing what was coming next.

In a new twist, I also gave candy to my son when he came up with questions for his sister and father. Asking questions is as much a skill as answering them, and perhaps even more valuable. From that point on, asking an intelligent question earned the same number of candies as answering one.

Both my daughter and my husband have followed in my son's footsteps by choosing books for our list as well. An added bonus of having so many people choose the reading material is that it exposes the rest of the family to literature and authors we might not have picked.

My son would not have chosen the *Just Grace* series by Charise Mericle Harper. But my daughter loves them. Even though my son complained at first, we told him that he had to respect her choice. And I think the sense of humor and clever artwork in this series sparked my son's imagination in a new way.

I'm not sure my daughter would have chosen *Ender's Game* by Orson Scott Card, one of the few books that my husband had read and loved. My husband's choice exposed my daughter to science fiction, which is not her favorite genre. But I know she enjoyed the novel and will be much more open to reading other science fiction novels in the future.

Having our children choose reading material also exposes them to different levels of literature. Sometimes, the book is a challenging step up, and sometimes it's a relaxing step down. There are benefits to both.

Our list of books has come from novels that I'm familiar with, suggestions from my husband, son, and daughter, recommendations from others, and looking through book lists that I've been able to find in libraries and online.

I'm always on the hunt for a good book.

# 8  CHOOSING CONTROVERSIAL BOOKS

I'm extremely picky about the books that we read as a family.

I'm proud of the titles that are on our list, and I'm equally proud of the titles that are not on our list.

For example, I refuse to read a book that shows kids treating each other rudely, and then promotes that behavior as funny or cool. I also refuse to read a book that mocks or belittles parents, teachers or other authority figures.

But that doesn't mean that I agree with all of the subject matter in the literature we've chosen. In fact, I have selected some of our reading material *specifically* because it contains content that I disagree with or want to work through.

When my son came home in the Second Grade already halfway through the first book from the Harry Potter series, I didn't think he was ready for it.

The series starts with light-hearted fare as Harry sets off to a magical school with an unusual set of teachers and an even more unusual set of courses and activities. But the subject material quickly becomes more mature. When a character kills and drinks the blood of a pure and defenseless unicorn in order to stay alive, the act is described as monstrous. I agree.

These are serious spiritual matters. Later books delve into the importance of blood in a ceremony/potion, the concept that murder splits the soul, the principle that only remorse can repair a shattered soul, and the power of a willing sacrifice. In my opinion, these are not subjects to be glossed over or taken lightly, and I wanted to be able to address them with my children.

I asked my son not to read the books and promised that when he was older, he would get a chance. To my son's credit, he did stop reading the series. I'm very proud of him for that choice, as it's not easy to put down a captivating book when you're in the middle of it. I am so grateful that he trusted me. A few years later, I kept my word, and we read the series together as a family.

When we told a few people that we would be reading the Harry Potter series, we received some rather strong caution from those who thought it was a poor choice. There was concern that the books glorified witchcraft and made it seem appealing. We considered carefully what was said.

We chose to go ahead with the books for two reasons. First, my children are going to be exposed to many different religions and philosophies. My husband and I want the opportunity to offer guidance and instruction as our children form their worldview, helping them to reason through their beliefs and values.

The second reason we chose to read the series came down to a simple question. How do we teach our children the skill of discernment?

I think it's a good question. Life is not always black and white. Things are rarely 'all good' or 'all bad'. How do we teach our children to recognize and distinguish between shades of grey? I saw the Harry Potter series as a great opportunity.

For example, the intricate plots in the Harry Potter series are full of wonderful fantasy and imagination. It is an inspiring story of friendship, loyalty, strength and courage. There are moments of such wonder that they brought tears to my eyes.

But the books also deal with spiritual matters that are very real, such as the power of blood, witchcraft, murder, sacrifice and repentance.

I wanted my children to enjoy the story and the positive values, but still be able to critically identify, question and analyze the portions that touched on our faith.

So, we read the entire series together. The final book coincided with a long road trip. Despite being stiff and weary from over five hours of car travel, we were enjoying the novel so much that we would have driven further just to keep reading. When we arrived at home, we sat in the car, on the driveway, and read until we finished the book.

Once we finished the series, I asked myself if we'd made the right decision, for our family, to read through these books. I believe that we did. We worked through subjects of great significance, and some of our deepest conversations have been sparked by these novels.

Later, my daughter wanted to read through the Warriors series by Erin Hunter. I was very uncomfortable with the emphasis on receiving guidance from the spirits of departed cats. But my husband felt it was important to 'demystify' subjects that our children will be exposed to outside the home. He saw our reading as an opportunity to influence the earliest perceptions of our children while removing any hype or attraction to the unknown.

So we proceeded and worked through all six books. However, we chose not to read beyond the first series. We felt that later books became darker and more involved with the afterlife, and the negativity outweighed the benefits of reading further.

Another series we worked through was the "How to Train Your Dragon" series by Cressida Cowell. I didn't agree with the emphasis on fate and didn't care for some of the adolescent humor with names like Snotface Snotlout, Dogsbreath the Duhbrain, and Big-Boobied Bertha. However, this book has some of the most powerful examples of loyalty, perseverance, friendship, courage, and forgiveness. There are several moments that moved me to tears. I didn't want to throw away the entire series, losing those amazing moments, because of a few names. The matter of fate was more serious, but again, we saw this as an opportunity to discuss alternate approaches to life while clarifying our own faith.

I'm happy to share that this series has become one of our absolute favorites. I've read it at least four times and my children have read it more. It is my daughter's favorite gift to give to friends.

The Hunger Games trilogy was another set of books that caused us to pause before we picked them up. As with much popular young adult fiction, the subject material can be dark and violent. The plot line of kids being forced to fight each other to the death is disturbing. However, the author, Suzanne Collins, chose not to be graphic in her description of the violence and didn't glorify killing. The books are filled with redeeming themes of perseverance, resourcefulness, friendship, family ties, loyalty, and self-sacrifice. My husband and I felt that our kids were mature enough to handle the material and, judging from the depth and quality of our conversations, we believe we made the right decision.

As a parent, I want my children to feel comfortable talking to me about any subject, even if they know I might disapprove. By reading books like this together, it gives us a chance to discuss all sorts of topics that simply don't come up in a regular day. The kids are free to question, doubt and disagree, and they still receive candy for expressing themselves.

We have enjoyed these 'controversial' books as much as, and even more, than some of the other books that might contain less questionable material.

Do I think that everyone should read controversial or questionable material? No. It's a choice for each family to make. We didn't take our decision lightly and have approached each of these series with much care and prayer.

There are many popular but controversial books that we won't be reading with our children and will strongly discourage them from reading. We don't want to read all questionable material, but we also don't want to throw out all such material either. We're trying to pick strategic books that we can use as an opportunity to discuss a variety of beliefs and perspectives on life.

I see it as my privilege and duty as a parent to guide my children as they explore various philosophies and worldviews. However, my upmost goal is to teach them to navigate for themselves. I am very proud of our conversations, and the depth of insight, understanding and discernment that my children have developed. I believe they are building a solid foundation for their values and faith.

I'm glad we chose to read these books.

## 9 CREATING QUESTIONS

When we first set out to read one book together as a family, I didn't plan to ask questions. My only plan was to read. But then *Roar!* came along with its ready-made set of chapter questions, and changed everything.

Once we finished with The Chronicles of Narnia, we had to decide if we would keep asking questions or drop them.

That was an easy decision for us. The kids loved the candy, and I loved our family discussions. We chose to keep the questions. But suddenly I was on my own, without a helpful resource.

Looking back now, I realize how fortunate it was that we began reading with a resource like *Roar!*. It served as a tutorial, instructing me in the art of asking questions.

I've come to believe there's no such thing as a 'bad' question. There's a place for simple questions that check basic understanding and answer the "who, what, when, where, why" of the plot and characters. There's also a place for deeper questions that require more thought and effort.

For me, the goal has been to ask both types - the simple as well as the more complex. This seemed to be easier with some books than others.

The easiest questions to ask are the ones that center on facts from the book, usually about the plot and characters. We call these 'one candy questions'.

Questions that involve more effort would be those that draw out opinions, ask for predictions, require analysis, or call for a personal connection. We call these 'two candy' or 'big candy' questions.

The following are some generic examples of questions that can be asked with most books.

*Has that ever happened to you?*
*Why do you think the character said or did that?*
*Was that a good choice?*
*What would you have done?*
*Do you agree? Who do you think was right?*
*Does this remind you of anyone/anything else?*

Is it necessary to ask questions while reading? No, although there are some great benefits.

For our family, asking questions changed the way that we listened. It kept everyone engaged. Searching for answers deepened our understanding of the novels we read and helped us to become better analytical thinkers. The conversations that have sprung from the questions have also broadened our understanding of ourselves, each other and the world.

The questions made us work harder. But we've been paid in full for our efforts, with candy, increased comprehension and conversation that has strengthened our connection to each other.

## 10  CELEBRATING SUCCESS

It took us a long time to read through one hundred books. Four years, to be exact.

Throughout those years, there have been books that have dragged, and seasons when we've read far less due to the busyness and distractions of life. There have also been times of discouragement, when we wondered if we would make our goal.

I have intentionally searched for ways to keep the momentum going. The candy was most helpful, but we found other strategies along the way that encouraged us to keep pushing forward.

1. I kept a current list of books that we'd finished taped to a cupboard. (My mother warned me that this was not a wise idea, as the tape will leave a residue. She's right, but it seemed the easiest way to post the list.)

   This list served as a visual reminder of our progress. We celebrated each small step while watching the page fill up. It also served as an incentive to keep adding more titles.

2. When friends came to our home, they often asked about the list. I had my kids explain, which gave them a chance to hear the compliments that usually followed.

3. We taped symbolic pictures on the fridge or cupboards (once again, to my mother's chagrin).

For example, there is an amazing moment in *Where the Red Fern Grows* where the main character, Billy, faces a near impossible task. He promised his dogs that if they put a raccoon up a tree, he'd chop it down. Old Dan and Little Ann came through, chasing a coon up the largest tree in the area. Billy came through as well, although it took days of determined effort and pushing through exhaustion, discouragement, and hands covered in painful blisters. I confess that I cried when the tree came down.

Once I wiped the tears away, I printed a picture of a huge tree and stuck it on our fridge. It's still there, as a symbolic reminder that we all face challenges that seem impossible. However, if we keep working at it and don't give up, with a little help, those big trees will fall.

While reading *Ungifted* by Gordon Korman, my daughter drew a hilarious picture of one of the characters, Noah, who misinterpreted a teacher's instructions and wore a ridiculous outfit to a school dance. I was thrilled that my daughter had formed such a strong visual while we'd been reading, and even more thrilled that she took the time to draw it. We tacked her artwork up beside our reading list as a reminder of a fun incident in a great book.

4. I regularly updated grandparents on our progress because they are some of the best cheerleaders around, always ready to champion our goals. Their praise and encouragement served as a verbal candy to the kids.

# 11  PASSING ON THE FAITH

I believe that one of the roles of a parent is to be deliberate. If we want out children to develop certain character traits, like honesty, compassion, kindness, and generosity, then we deliberately need to encourage those traits.

One of the most important things that I want to pass on to my children is my spiritual faith. This is so very important because what we believe is foundational and provides direction for the decisions we will make in life. I don't want to force my beliefs. But through word and example, I want to model my faith so that my kids can make their own choice.

Reading together has given my husband and me the opportunity to discuss what we believe and why we believe it. We have deliberately chosen books such as *Little Pilgrim's Progress* by Helen L. Taylor, *The Cross and the Switchblade* by David Wilkerson, *Vanya* by Myrna Grant, and *Dinner with a Perfect Stranger* by David Gregory, in order to discuss our values and beliefs. As stated earlier, we have also chosen books that do not share our beliefs, and we have respectfully read and discussed these as well.

Our family has devotions together every morning. For a long time, we bounced back and forth between working through devotional books and reading various portions of the Bible. Then, my husband suggested we read through the entire Bible as a family.

I confess that I wasn't so keen on the idea at first. There are some dry books, like Leviticus and Deuteronomy. There are also some confusing books, like Isaiah and Revelation. I wasn't sure how engaged my children would be, especially first thing in the morning.

But the more I thought about it, the more I realized that it was the single most important thing that we could do with our children.

So, we began to read through the entire Bible together. I realized I needed help, so I pulled out a Quest Bible Study Guide to serve as a resource. It contains helpful explanations in a sidebar running the length of each page, which I consulted frequently.

There are sections of the Bible that are troubling and confusing. In fact, there are many times when I ask a question and the response I'm looking for is, "I don't know". That response earns a candy because we don't understand everything and shouldn't be afraid to admit it.

I can think of no greater gift or treasure that I can pass on to my kids than to work through the entire Bible with them. I hope it will build a foundation of faith and a heart of wonder and praise.

In case you're wondering, we will be counting the Bible as only one book on our list, even though there are 66 books within it. I confess that I'm seriously tempted to count each of them individually. But somehow it feels like that would be cheating, so we'll keep to the straight and narrow and count the Bible as a single book.

## 12  WE DID IT!

We did it!

We read one hundred books together as a family. It took four years and over a thousand hours. Probably far more. But we reached our goal.

I am so happy that we took this journey. The experience has surpassed everything I had expected or hoped.

What did we do to celebrate? We went to the bookstore, of course, and everyone bought a book. The kids also chose a few other fun non-book items. Normally, I might have refused but I was feeling rather generous after our huge accomplishment. I'm sure the kids knew that and made the most of it.

One of my hopes is that the kids will read many of these books again and again. It would be a tragedy to read a book like *To Kill a Mockingbird* by Harper Lee only once. I feel that way about so many of the novels. Personally, I try to read through The Chronicles of Narnia and The Lord of the Rings series by J. R. R. Tolkien at least once a year. These novels have become familiar friends, and I treasure spending time with them. I'm hoping that my children will feel the same, and spend time in the future getting reacquainted with their favorite books.

## 13  DID I ACHIEVE MY GOAL?

Now that we've arrived at our destination, it's time for reflection.

Has all the time, effort, and candy been worth it?

Yes!

Did I achieve my goal and turn my children into avid readers?

Yes . . . mostly!

My children are reading much more on their own. Perhaps they aren't as crazy about books as I was when I was a child, but they are definitely eager readers. I am thrilled.

Not only are they reading more, but they're reading better. As their comprehension, fluency, and decoding skills have increased, so has their enjoyment.

Has it worked out exactly as I planned?

No! It's worked out better. And the surprises along the way have been the best part of all.

One of the greatest surprises has been my husband. I really can't exaggerate what a poor reader he was when we began.

My husband didn't read much as a child, and this continued throughout his teenage years. He should have flunked his Eleventh Grade English class, and only passed due to the generous mercy of his teacher.

When we first began to read, my husband didn't answer a lot of questions or earn many candies. But over time, he has become incredibly intuitive and analytical. He's adding thoughtful insights to the conversations, and picking up on answers quicker than the kids. That was not happening at the beginning. Of course, he's rubbing it in. And I don't mind because he's earned the right to do so.

Another surprise is the number of 'inside' or 'private' family jokes that we have. When my son mows the lawn without being asked, and I say, "Azalea", he knows what I mean. When my daughter helps me with the dishes, or cleans her room, and I tell her "Chrysanthemum", she understands. You would understand too, if you'd read *The Wednesday Wars* by Gary D. Schmidt, which you may want to read just so you don't look like a pied ninny (another reference from *The Wednesday Wars*).

The other day, my son had a small present to give to his grandma. Instead of just handing it to her, he asked, "What have I got in my pocketses?" and followed up with a few other riddles before presenting her with the gift. Grandma loved the present, and the clever reference to Gollum from *The Hobbit* by J. R. R. Tolkien.

When things happen that we don't understand, we also like to remind each other that God isn't a tame lion, which makes complete sense if you've read *The Lion, the Witch and the Wardrobe* by C. S. Lewis.

The kids are continually coming up with phrases or incidents from books we've read. They've become masters of allusions, and I love it. Of course, these references always earn a candy. Sometimes even a big one!

Another unexpected outcome of reading together is that the books have kept us talking. We began with children in elementary school and finished with two kids in college. We haven't escaped the typical issues that come as our kids have transitioned into teenagers and young adults. Moodiness, arguments, and pushing back on rules – we've got it all.

But although the teen years are often characterized as a time when sharing between parents and kids happens *less*, we've been talking *more* than ever. And laughing. And depending on the book, crying. Well, that's usually me. I'm the crier in the family.

The other night, my daughter wasn't in the best of moods, and had retreated to her room. When I called her to come for our evening reading, she refused. I didn't argue. I simply told her that Lucas would be coming home, and we'd find out what Principal Peattie had said to Doug Swieteck. She joined us immediately, without further protest. We worked through an emotional section of the book, and my daughter's chin quivered as we read about Lucas and how he looked different. When we finished, my daughter participated fully in the conversation, and all traces of moodiness had vanished.

Reading can calm and touch the heart of a melancholy teen. I watched it with my daughter that night. This is especially true if it's a fabulous novel like *Okay for Now* by Gary D. Schmidt, which you'll have to read for yourself to find out what Principal Peattie said and why my daughter felt so sad when Lucas came home.

When we first began, I thought we were going to read books. And we did. But it's about more than books.

It's about the hours and hours of time together. We have talked our way through all sorts of situations in books, and all sorts of issues in our own lives.

I can't imagine where our family would be if we hadn't read together. So many laughs we would have missed, so many life-changing conversations, and so much sharing of our lives. Our family is closer, and our bonds are stronger, because we've read together.

Yes, I have achieved my goals...and so much more.

## 14 THINGS I WISH I'D DONE DIFFERENTLY

No journey is perfect, and we've had our fair share of stumbles. If I could go back to the beginning, there are several things that I would have done differently.

1.  I wish I'd recorded the exact day we started reading. At the time, I thought we'd only be reading one book. I had no idea how it would grow. I know my son was in Fourth Grade and my daughter was in Second Grade. But I wish I had a specific start date.

2.  I wish I'd recorded the exact day we finished.

3.  I wish I'd logged all the hours we've read. We read 142 books, and I can guess, as a low estimate, that we've read at least one thousand hours. Probably far more. But I'd really like to know for sure.

4.  I wish I'd kept the exact order of the books as we read them.

    When I began, the list was in order. But some of the series that we were reading hadn't been completed. For example, when we read *Swindle* by Gordon Korman, we had no idea that more would follow. We worked through a few other books, and then *Zoobreak*, the second in the series, was published. It made sense to rearrange the list so that *Swindle* and *Zoobreak* stayed together. That kept the series intact but changed the order of my list.

Another problem came when I tried to fit one hundred titles on the same page. I had to rearrange again, in order to make it work. So, I have a complete list of the books, but not the order in which they were read.

I wish I had kept two lists, one with the correct order, and one with the series listed together, fitting neatly on a single page.

# 15  HELPFUL HINTS

We chose a goal on the far horizon, one hundred books, and started walking toward it. There was no path to follow, and we had to figure things out as we went along. Some of our ideas worked better than others. Here are a few of the better ideas.

1.  I pre-read all the books so that I was familiar with the story and could ask questions. This took a lot of work and is one of the reasons why I give myself free candies. I figure that I've earned them by pre-reading the books. I confess that I'm quite generous to myself.

2.  We usually don't watch movies based on books, especially if the movie has made significant changes to the main plot. It bothers me when the movie doesn't follow the book upon which it is based. I get even more frustrated when the movie makes massive changes to the plot and characters. I want to yell at the producers, "You have the book. You're making a movie based on the book. Follow it!"

    However, there are some advantages to watching a movie that has done a poor job of adapting the book. I smile when I hear my children complain that a movie left out crucial parts of the book. I break out into a happy dance when my children say, "The book was so much better than the movie." That's music to my ears!

3.   It doesn't have to be one person doing all the reading. My son, daughter and husband have all taken turns reading.

For those who don't like to read aloud, there are books on tape or CD. We've never used them because I like the freedom to stop and comment in 'real-time'.

As a word of encouragement to those who struggle with reading aloud, it's a skill like any other. Practice will bring improvement. And don't forget to reward yourself with candy for your efforts.

4.   We have found reading at the dinner table to be one of the best times to work through books. Much research has been done about the value of families that share meals together, and I love that my kids will often stay long after their plates are empty, just so I can finish a section or chapter.

However, reading at the dinner table does make it hard for me to get through the meal. I usually start eating early, snatch quick bites while the others answer questions, and still end up finishing last. My food gets cold and rushing through the meal probably isn't the best for digestion. But I see it as a small and noble sacrifice for my family. It also gives me another reason to reward myself with candy.

5.   There's a simple reason why candy has worked so well as a motivator in my family. My kids don't get a lot of sweets. Candy is a scarce resource, and they're willing to work hard to earn it.

But it's not necessary to motivate with edible rewards. The key is to find what's valuable to your kids. As my children have grown older, we've had to adjust our rewards. We've switched to larger prizes, like computer time and monetary rewards.

Above all, the physical prize is just a token. The recognition, the approval and the compliments are far more valuable.

6.  Someone recently asked me if my kids read without candy. Yes, absolutely. Just because we're reading together as a family doesn't mean that they can stop reading on their own. It's important for them to have novels that they read independently.

    When we read together, my children still want some type of reward for their answering and insights. But they're reading far more on their own, without any external motivation. They read because they enjoy it, and that is its own reward.

7.  Our reading list also serves as a gift guide that works for all ages, young or old. The added bonus is that all the book gifts come with our personal stamp of approval.

    My daughter was recently invited to two birthday parties. For each of them, she asked me to buy her friends the first few books in the "How To Train Your Dragon" series by Cressida Cowell. I was pleased, until I saw the card she wrote. Then, I was thrilled.

    My daughter had created a mosaic of a Viking ship riding the crest of a huge wave. At the top of the page, she wrote a special quote from the novels, "A hero is forever". This was followed by a lengthy card, in which she wrote about how her friend could be a 'hero forever'.

In my opinion, that was an amazing gift. I couldn't have been prouder to watch my daughter work so hard to share a book and a message that meant a lot to her.

# 16  THINGS TO CONSIDER

1.  I try to interest my children not only in books, but also in the authors who wrote them. The lives of authors are often as interesting and inspirational as the stories they write.

    Did you know that Gordon Kormon published his first novel at the age of fourteen, or that Carl Hiaasen has been writing ever since his father gave him a typewriter at the age of six?

    Did you know that as a young girl, Cressida Cowell was fascinated with dragons? Our copy of *How to Train Your Dragon* has a photo of a nine-year-old Cressida, sitting on a small island off the coast of Scotland, writing stories. Who knew that many years later, she would write a twelve-book series that would inspire three major movies...all about dragons.

    I want my children to be fascinated and inspired by these authors. Who knows what book, invention, or company is growing within my kids right now, just waiting to burst out?

    I haven't had to search far to find information about the authors. Many books give a brief biography on the inside cover or back flap, and some also have a 'Question and Answer' section at the end.

We went a step farther and wrote to two of our favorite authors. My son wrote to Gordon Korman (*This Can't Be Happening at MacDonald Hall* and *Swindle* series, among others) through his Scholastic address. My daughter wrote to Charise Mericle Harper (*Just Grace* series, among others) through her website. We felt it was important to thank them and let them know how much we enjoyed their books.

I am pleased to report that we received wonderful letters back (and a few treats) from both authors. I think it was a special moment of connection for my kids and made them appreciate the books even more.

2.  Reading and writing are often linked together. In an interview printed at the back of our copy of *The Outsiders* (platinum edition), S. E. Hinton was asked what made her want to become a writer. She said the major influence on her writing was her reading, which she did all the time. By the way, she was a fifteen-year-old high school student when she began writing her first book, and received a contract from a publisher on graduation day.

I'm beginning to see the influence of our reading in my daughter's writing. She's writing more, and she's writing better. My son has no love for pen and paper and is an absolute minimalist when it comes to written assignments. But the potential is there. I can hear the difference that our reading has made in his speech, vocabulary, and reasoning. I believe the writing skills will come through when he needs them.

If a child wants to become a writer, the best preparation they can do is to read, read, and then read more.

3.    My son thrives when it comes to Math, Science, and Computer courses, but not so much in English class. He doesn't find it as easy or enjoyable. But that doesn't mean he gets a pass when it comes to reading fiction. In fact, reading fiction may be one of the best ways for him to prepare for a future in the technical subjects that he loves.

In a fascinating article entitled 'Face facts: we need fiction', Neil Gaiman relates a conversation with a top official at the first party-approved science fiction and fantasy convention in China in 2007. Mr. Gaiman questioned the official about the change in attitude toward science fiction. The official explained that the Chinese were brilliant at following plans, but didn't innovate or invent. So they sent a delegation to the United States in order to talk with individuals at successful companies like Apple, Microsoft and Google, who were responsible for inventing the future. They discovered that all of these top creative minds read science fiction when they were younger. That realization was the key that opened the door in China for science fiction and fantasy novels.

If I could give a message to all young computer techies, science geeks and math nerds (terms I use with great affection as I married one and am raising another), it would be this. Read fiction! It is through fantasy and science fiction that the impossible becomes possible, and these novels will play a critical role in molding an innovative, creative and successful mind. Fiction is good for you.

4.    My daughter has been disappointed with school lately. I've been disappointed as well, and disturbed. It's not because of her teachers, because they have been fabulous. It's not because of the schools, because my children are fortunate to

attend wonderful public schools. It's because of the changing curriculum.

For years, my daughter watched her older brother create amazing projects for book reports, and she looked forward to getting her chance to do the same. But things have been different for her. As she moves up each year, we've found that a concerning number of book reports, classroom reading contests, and other creative year-long literacy assignments have been disappearing from the curriculum.

Again, this isn't the fault of teachers. The curriculum is placing an increasingly heavy emphasis on non-fiction reading while decreasing the amount of time spent with classical and fictional literature. The opportunity for creative projects based on books has also been decreasing.

I want my children to be filled with imagination, curiosity and empathy. These traits are sparked and nourished by fiction. If school curriculum is reducing fiction, then we need to encourage it all the more at home.

5.  Reading can make a difference in academic success in all grades and subjects.

In *Gifted Hands*, Ben Carson wrote of the importance of books in his life. Ben was a failing fifth grade student with the odds stacked against him when his mother turned off the television and sent him to the library, requiring weekly book reports. To make a long and successful story short, he read his way to becoming the Director of Pediatric Neurosurgery at John Hopkins Hospital. He's now retired from the medical field, and competed to be a candate for president of the United States in the 2016 election. Ben Carson traces his success back to several factors, and chief among them is . . . reading books.

I highly doubt that my children will pursue pediatric neurosurgery or run for president, and that's fine with me. I'm not so concerned with what they pursue, but rather that they choose to pursue something. When they find that goal, I want them to be equipped to succeed. Ben Carson is living proof that reading can play a critical part in attaining one's goals.

6.  As my children have grown, I've learned that they don't need me *less*. They need me *different*. I would even say they need my guidance *more* than ever, although I have to be careful how I give it. Reading together has given my husband and me an indirect way to be involved, present and speaking into the lives of our children, even as they transitioned into teenagers and then young adults.

    There are great benefits to reading with your children when they're young. But there are also great benefits to reading together when they're older.

7.  Even if your family chooses not to read 100 books aloud together, it's a great idea to encourage your child to set a personal goal to read a set number of books. Keep track of the progress with a list posted in a public place in your home, and cheerlead for them, celebrating success in a big way when the goal is met.

## 17 CRAZY PLACES WE'VE READ

One of the great things about books is that they're portable and can be taken just about anywhere. We've read in a lot of fun places.

Anytime that our family is all together in the car, we're reading. In fact, we've purposely gone on road trips just so we could read. Driving back in the evening when it's dark doesn't stop us. I turn on the passenger light and just keep going.

We've read on a floating gazebo at a lake, with the sun setting and sounds of nature all around.

We've read on an airplane, huddled together and trying to listen over the hum of engines.

We've read at a nearby park, sprawled out on the play structure and soaking in the sun.

We've read in restaurants, competing with music while trying to be respectful of other guests.

We've read in a variety of hotel rooms while relaxing on vacation.

We've found ways to create variety in our home environment. Our favorite is to warm blankets in the dryer, wrap ourselves in them, light a fire, and I serve chocolate-covered strawberries while we sit on the floor in the living room, listening to our current book.

The reason that I used to read so much as a child was because I enjoyed it. I have done everything I can to make reading enjoyable for my family. It's working. How do I know? Because when we get in the car, before I even fasten my seatbelt, my son usually asks, "Did you bring the book? Can you read?"

My answer is, "Yes, but safety first. Give me just a minute to buckle up."

## 18 NOT DONE YET

I have an announcement to make.

We're not done yet!

After we finished our 100th book, we voted unanimously not to stop. We're going to keep going, and we've set a new goal of reading 200 books together.

I am so glad that we've kept reading, because if we hadn't, we wouldn't have discovered our new favorite author, Gary D. Schmidt. We've just finished three of his books – *The Wednesday Wars* (book #103), *Trouble* (#108), and *Okay For Now* (#110). I know there are other books and authors just waiting for us to discover them.

Are we going to make it to two hundred books? I don't know.

Don't tell my kids, but I really don't care. I am just thankful for every minute that we spend together.

# 19  OTHER FAMILY ACTIVITIES

If I could pick only one word to describe the job of parenting, it would be "deliberate". Or "intentional". I know that's more than one word, but I think we can let it slide because they mean the same thing.

I believe that parents need to be deliberate about spending *quality* and *quantity* time together with their kids. We need to be intentional about passing on the qualities, traits and lessons we believe are valuable.

Reading books together has been a fabulous way for my husband and me to deliberately invest in our kids. But as great as reading books has been, we've come up with a few other fun things to do together.

1.   We love to carry our kitchen table into the living room and position it right in front of the TV. Then, we eat supper together and watch shows like Shark Tank, Undercover Boss, Brain Games and select episodes of Judge Judy.

I like these shows because they're entertaining, but also cover practical issues like investments, career choices, risk-taking, legal matters, and work ethics. I eat with a fork in one hand and the remote in the other so I can pause the show while we make predictions and discuss decisions. I rarely get through an episode of Undercover Boss without a few tears rolling down my cheeks. The kids laugh, but I don't mind. In my own defense, I think that the longer I live, the more ugliness and disappointment I see in the world. When I see beauty, courage and strength, I appreciate it so much more, and it moves me to tears.

By the way, if you haven't cried during a really good book, then I suggest you keep reading until you do. It's something everyone should experience at least once.

2.   We love to play board games and hold tournaments, especially when the grandparents come to visit. I make up a huge chart/bracket, and then we play Connect Four or Blokus as if our lives depended on it. And, you guessed it, I tape the charts up on our cupboards (as my mother looks the other way).

My kitchen certainly wouldn't win any contests for its stylish decor, but I like to think that it shines with a personal touch.

## 20 THE LIST

I'm very proud of our reading list. But it isn't perfect.

Perhaps we could have read more classics. Or maybe we could have picked more biographies. But there's a reason behind every choice, and each one has meant something to our family.

The list isn't perfect. But it's ours. We have enjoyed some books more than others. And some we have loved.

I'm including a copy of our list at the end of this book, not because it's what everyone should read, but because it's a guide to possibility.

## 21 A FAVORITE QUOTE

That are many great quotes about reading, but I'm going to exercise self-control and share just one – my absolute favorite.

*"I would be content if my children grew up to be the kind of people who think interior decorating consists mostly of building enough bookshelves."* Anna Quindlen

I feel the same.

## 22 FINAL THOUGHTS

You probably guessed that I would end with a challenge, and you'd be right. But I'm not going to challenge you to read one hundred books. Is that a relief?

I would like to challenge your family to read one book aloud together.

It can be read with or without questions. With or without candy. And it can be whichever book you choose. (Although I highly recommend *The Lion, the Witch and the Wardrobe* as a good place to start.)

Maybe you'll stop after one book. Maybe you'll read more. Maybe you'll choose something entirely different.

Just remember that it's about more than books.

If you do something and do it together, you'll create moments and memories that will last a lifetime. Best of all, you will bond with your children and transform your family.

# 23   OUR LIST

1. *Little Pilgrim's Progress* by Helen L. Taylor
2. *The Magician's Nephew* by C. S. Lewis
3. *The Lion, The Witch & the Wardrobe* by C. S. Lewis
4. *Prince Caspian* by C. S. Lewis
5. *The Horse and His Boy* by C. S. Lewis
6. *Voyage of the Dawn Treader* by C. S. Lewis
7. *The Silver Chair* by C. S. Lewis
8. *The Last Battle* by C. S. Lewis
9. *Charlie and The Chocolate Factory* by Roald Dahl
10. *How To Train Your Dragon* by Cressida Cowell
11. *How to be a Pirate* by Cressida Cowell
12. *How to Speak Dragonese* by Cressida Cowell
13. *How to Cheat a Dragon's Curse* by Cressida Cowell
14. *How to Twist a Dragon's Tale* by Cressida Cowell
15. *A Hero's Guide to Deadly Dragons* by Cressida Cowell
16. *How to Ride a Dragon's Storm* by Cressida Cowell
17. *How to Break a Dragon's Heart* by Cressida Cowell
18. *How to Steal a Dragon's Sword* by Cressida Cowell
19. *How to Seize a Dragon's Jewel* by Cressida Cowell
20. *How to Betray a Dragon's Hero* by Cressida Cowell
21. *How to Fight a Dragon's Fury* by Cressida Cowell
22. *Swindle* by Gordon Korman
23. *Zoobreak* by Gordon Korman
24. *Framed* by Gordon Korman
25. *Showoff* by Gordon Korman
26. *Hideout* by Gordon Korman

27. *Jackpot* by Gordon Korman
28. *Unleashed* by Gordon Korman
29. *Book One: Shipwreck* by G. Korman
30. *Book Two: Survival* by Gordon Korman
31. *Book Three: Escape* by Gordon Korman
32. *Ramona the Pest* by Beverly Cleary
33. *The Voyages of Doctor Dolittle* by Hugh Lofting
34. *Holes* by Louis Sachar
35. *Just Grace* by Charise Mericle Harper
36. *Still Just Grace* by Charise Mericle Harper
37. *Just Grace Walks the Dog* by Charise Mericle Harper
38. *Just Grace and Snack Attack* by Charise Mericle Harper
39. *Just Grace Goes Green* by Charise Mericle Harper
40. *Just Grace and the Terrible Tutu* by C. M Harper
41. *Just Grace and the Double Surprise* by C. M. Harper
42. *Just Grace, Star on Stage* by Charise Mericle Harper
43. *Just Grace & the Trouble with Cupcakes* by C. M. Harper
44. *39 Clues – Book 1 – The Maze of Bones* by Rick Riordan
45. *39 Clues – Book 2 – One False Note* by Gordon Korman
46. *39 Clues – Book 3 – The Sword Thief* by Peter Lerangis
47. *39 Clues – Book 4 – Beyond the Grave* by Jude Watson
48. *39 Clues – Book 5 – The Black Circle* by Patrick Carman
49. 39 Clues – Book 6 – In Too Deep by Jude Watson
50. 39 Clues – Book 7 – The Viper's Nest by Peter Lerangis
51. *39 Clues – Book 8 – The Emperor's Code* by Gordon Korman
52. *39 clues – Book 9 – Storm Warning* by Linda Sue Park
53. *39 clues – Book 10 – Into the Gauntlet* by M. P. Haddix
54. *This Can't Be Happening at MacDonald Hall* Gordon Korman
55. *Go Jump in the Pool!* By Gordon Korman
56. *Beware the Fish!* By Gordon Korman
57. *The War with Mr. Wizzle* by Gordon Korman
58. *The Zucchini Warriors* by Gordon Korman

59. *Lights, Camera, Disaster!* by Gordon Korman
60. *Something's Fishy at MacDonald Hall* by Gordon Korman
61. *Ella Enchanted* by Gail Carson Levine
62. *Radio 5th Grade* by Gordon Korman
63. *Marian's Big Book of Bible Stories* by Marian Schoolland
64. *Harry Potter and the Sorcerer's Stone* by J.K. Rowling
65. *Harry Potter and the Chamber of Secrets* by J. K. Rowling
66. *Harry Potter and the Prisoner of Azkhaban* by J. K. Rowling
67. *Harry Potter and the Goblet of Fire* by J. K. Rowling
68. *Harry Potter and the Order of the Phoenix* by J. K. Rowling
69. *Harry Potter and the Half-Blood Prince* by J. K. Rowling
70. *Harry Potter and the Deathly Hallows* by J. K. Rowling
71. *Mr. Popper's Penguins* by Richard & Florence Atwater
72. *I want to go Home* by Gordon Korman
73. *UnGifted* by Gordon Korman
74. *The Best Christmas Pageant Ever* Barbara Robinson
75. *The Best School Year Ever* Barbara Robinson
76. *Where the Red Fern Grows* by Wilson Rawls
77. *Where the Mountain Meets the Moon* Grace Lin
78. One-Way Bible
79. *God's Smuggler* by Brother Andrew
80. *Watership Down* by Richard Adams
81. *Hoot* by Carl Hiassen
82. *Warriors – Into the Wild* Erin Hunter
83. *Warriors – Fire and Ice* by Erin Hunter
84. *Warriors - Forest of Secrets* Erin Hunter
85. *Warriors – Rising Storm* by Erin Hunter
86. *Warriors – A Dangerous Path* by Erin Hunter
87. *Warriors – The Darkest Hour* by Erin Hunter
88. *The Fellowship of the Rings* by J. R. R. Tolkien
89. *The Two Towers* by J. R. R. Tolkien
90. *The Return of the King* by J. R. R. Tolkien
91. *The Hobbit* by J. R. R. Tolkien
92. *The Hunger Games* by Suzanne Collins

93. *Catching Fire* by Suzanne Collins
94. *Mockingjay* by Suzanne Collins
95. *Dinner with a Perfect Stranger* David Gregory
96. *A Day with a Perfect Stranger* David Gregory
97. *The Princess and the Goblin* George MacDonald
98. *The Princess and Curdie* George MacDonald
99. *To Kill a Mockingbird* by Harper Lee
100. *Don't Mess with Moses* by Marty Nystrom
101. *The Toothpaste Millionaire* by Jean Merrill
102. *Tuck Everlasting* by Natalie Babbitt
103. *The Wednesday Wars* by Gary D.Schmidt
104. *The CandyMakers* by Wendy Mass
105. *Vanya* by Myrna Grant
106. *The Boy on the Wooden Box* by Leon Leyson
107. *The Cross & the Switchblade* by David Wilkerson
108. *Trouble* by Gary D. Schmidt
109. *The Outsiders* by S. E. Hinton
110. *Okay for Now* by Gary D. Schmidt
111. *The Penderwicks* by Jeanne Birdsall
112. *Old Yeller* by Fred Gipson
113. *Summer of the Monkeys* by Wilson Rawls
114. *The Hiding Place* by Corrie ten Boom
115. *The Help* by Kathryn Stockett
116. *This Present Darkness* by Frank Peretti
117. *Flipped* by Wendelin Van Draanen
118. *Freak the Mighty* by Rodman Philbrick
119. *The One and Only Ivan* by Katherine Applegate
120. *Christy* by Catherine Marshall
121. *Night* by Elie Wiesel
122. *Of Mice and Men* by John Steinbeck
123. *The Purpose Driven Life* by Rick Warren
124. *A Semester in the Life of a Garbage Bag* by Gordon Korman
125. *The False Prince* by Jennifer A. Nielsen

126. *The Runaway King* by Jennifer A. Nielsen
127. *The Shadow Throne* by Jennifer A. Nielsen
128. *A Night Divided* by Jennifer A. Nielsen
129. *Ender's Game* by Orson Scott Card
130. *Ender's Shadow* by Orson Scott Card
131. *Speaker for the Dead* by Orson Scott Card
132. *Xenocide* by Orson Scott Card
133. *Children of the Mind* by Orson Scott Card
134. *Girls, Guys and a Tangle of Ties* by Galynne Matichuk
135. *Supergifted* by Gordon Kormon
136. *Fountainhead* by Ayn Rand
137. The Bible
138. *Pay Attention, Carter Jones* by Gary D. Schmidt
139. *Atlas Shrugged* by Ayn Rand (current novel)
140. *Pride and Prejudice* by Jane Austen
141. *Shadow of the Hegemon* by Orson Scott Card
142. *1984* by George Orwell

## 24  GOOD TIME FOR AN UPDATE

It's been five years since we reached the goal of reading one hundred books together as a family.

We started the journey when my son was in Fourth Grade and my daughter was in the 2nd grade. Nick is currently in his first year at a local college, and GrAce is in 11th grade.

It seemed like a good time for an update. Because we're still reading. And I have a few more thoughts to share.

*(As an additional update, we read together until my son and daughter moved away for university. But we still read when they came home for the summer!)*

# 25  THE MEGA CANDY

Some things never cease to amaze me. I marvel at the creativity (and/or greed) of my kids, especially when it involves candy or money. I delight in their enjoyment of a compliment.

The reward system started with a "Candy" reward for answering a question or sharing an insight. This was a very simple treat. A single jellybean or gummy bear for an intelligent comment. But that wasn't enough.

As an added incentive, we introduced the "Big Candy". The "Big Candy" is five small candies earned at once for a superior insight.

As money became more of an incentive, we converted each small candy to a tally mark worth five cents. A big candy earned a cash value of twenty-five cents. But even that was not enough.

My eighteen-year-old son recently proposed the "Mega Candy" reward. This reward is equal to five big candy rewards all at once. Or a total cash payout of $1.25.

It takes a truly brilliant observation to earn a Mega Candy Reward. The kids have each earned several thus far. My husband is working on it.

## 26 EXPOSURE

Some things are taught. More things are caught.

That's a great saying. It's clever. It rhymes. But most important of all, it's true. I have done my best to exposure my children to both.

I've worked hard not only to read with my children, but to read around them. I always have a book (or three) on the go.

I need to lead by example if I want my reading habits to be contagious. I discuss the books I'm reading, leave them lying around the house, carry them with me, and pull them out when waiting for an appointment instead of reaching for my phone.

I want to expose my kids to the habit of reading in the hope that they will catch a serious case of Bibliophagy - the act or habit of reading voraciously. And never recover.

## 27  PASSING ON THE FAITH...ROUND TWO

Every morning, while enjoying a breakfast of eggs or a homemade smoothie, we have our family devotion time. In the past, we bounced between various inspirational books and select passages from the Bible. Then my husband suggested that we read the entire Bible.

As I shared earlier, my initial reaction was not positive. It seemed a daunting and overwhelming challenge. But after thinking it through, I came to view it as one of the best goals we could set. And...

We did it. Cover to cover. Genesis to Revelation. And everything in between.

When I look over our list of books, the Bible is the title of which I am most proud.

When we decided to read through the Bible, I knew that it was a good plan. The right thing to do with our kids. No doubt about that. But the further we got in the Good Book, the more that I began to feel the enormity of our choice. And this was confirmed to me one morning as we read through Deuteronomy 6:4-8.

*Hear, O Israel: The LORD our God, the LORD is one. Love the LORD your God with all your heart and with all your soul and with all your strength. These commandments that I give you today are to be on your hearts. Impress them on your children. Talk about them when you sit at home and when you walk along the road, when you lie down and when you get up. Tie them as symbols on your hands and bind them on your foreheads. Write them on the doorframes of your houses and on your gates.*

Three things jumped out to me as we read that passage.

First, this is direct instruction from God to us.

We are to impress the Word of God on our children. It's not an option. Other versions translate impress as to teach diligently, carefully, to repeat and to tell.

This is a priority from God.

Second, we are to incorporate Biblical truth into daily routines.

Simply said? We make the most of every opportunity.

In Old Testament times, God gave the Israelites a plan. They were to talk about the commandments of God when they sat at home, when they walked along the road, and in the morning and at night.

And here I thought I was being original and rather clever – reading at meal times as we sat around the kitchen table, reading when we woke in the morning and when we tucked the kids in at night, reading while we drove in the car - as if I came up with some new thing. It was in the Bible all along.

God's plan is simple. It's open to everyone at every stage. We take the daily routines of life and deliberately infuse them with faith.

Third, passing on the faith is our purpose as parents.

We often delegate the job of teaching to the professionals in the school system or volunteers in our sports programs or churches. While these individuals have a valuable role to play, this passage makes it clear that parents are the primary teachers. We are to take responsibility for impressing the things of God in the hearts and minds of our children, and we're to make it natural and normal by including the Word of God in daily routines.

God's priority, His plan and His purpose – impressing the Word of God on our children.

It's done through deliberate, continual conversation during the common routines of the day.

This passage confirmed to me that by reading together as a family, both a variety of novels as well as daily reading of the Word of God, we're following God's commands, in the way God commanded, according to the job He gave us.

I felt great satisfaction when we finished Revelation and said "Amen". And I could almost hear the voice of God whispering, "Well done."

However, there was no question of what to do once we finished. Obviously, we'd start over and do it again. Right back to "In the beginning...". If the Bible is going to be a lamp to our feet and a light for our path, then we need to carry it ever before us.

I confess that we have made a few changes for "round two". We're skipping over the more technical chapters, such as building instructions for the tabernacle and the ceremonial Levitical laws. If you've read through the architectural blueprints, with instructions about pillars and pomegranates, you know what I mean.

We've also had to become more creative now that we're juggling high school, college and work schedules. There are mornings when I read with my daughter, send her off on the bus, dash upstairs to read the Bible to my son while he's still in bed, and then rush off to work.

I don't know if we'll finish reading through the Bible a second time. But I know this. As long as my kids are living in my home, it is my job, duty and privilege to make the most of every opportunity to impress the Word of God on their hearts, minds and souls.

## 28  RAP MUSIC AND VIDEO CONTESTS

It's hard to measure exactly how reading together has affected my kids. I know that the thousands of hours we've spent turning pages has changed us in significant ways. But how can I quantify the results? Sure, the kids have received excellent grades in Language Arts and Social Studies. But something happened over this summer that made me think about how unpredictable and far-reaching the influence might be.

While on his way to our church summer camp, my son learned there was going to be a talent contest. So he wrote a rap. While riding on a bumpy, noisy bus. Performed it the next day. And won the talent contest.

When he was telling me about the victory, my son acted like it was no big deal. He said that he didn't have a lot of competition. Which might have been true. But what impressed me wasn't his first-place finish. What impressed me was the ease of his writing.

Nick doesn't like to write in school. He considers essays a form of cruel and unusual punishment and puts in as little effort as possible. I hadn't thought about how the hours spent reading have affected Nick's writing until this contest. And while composing a rap may not compare to writing a formal essay, the rap still requires structure, rhythm, and rhyme. Not easy to pull off while riding on a noisy bus, full of distractions. But even under less-than-ideal circumstances, the writing just flowed out of him.

I am impressed that Nick was able to whip up a lyrical piece of poetry, and even if there weren't a lot of other serious contenders, his rap was strong enough to win.

But this wasn't my son's first attempt at writing. He's written rap songs for several school assignments. For example, he needed to write about Margaret Thatcher for an 11th grade History class, and he chose to use the form of a rap. The teacher was so impressed after he performed for his class, that she pulled him from his next class and had him come back and perform it again for her next set of students. He got an A on that assignment.

He also wrote a rap for his Robotics team, recorded an accompanying video, and posted it on Youtube. The rap is still played as a rallying song, even though he's moved on from the team.

Over the past three years he's written close to a hundred rap songs.

I never expected my son to write rap music. This is not how I thought our reading would influence his skills and abilities. But the writing seems to flow out of him, and he enjoys it.

He recently entered another contest. Students in his Video and Production class were assigned a themed project. The class winners were sent on to a district-wide contest. Nick wrote a striking poem, added simple yet powerful film footage, and came second in his category. It was extremely creative filming with a pointed poetic message.

There's no way to predict the rewards of reading. I am learning not to limit or be surprised at the ways that reading has impacted my children. And while I would prefer that my son not choose rap artist as a career, I recognize that he's talented at writing. If he ever becomes famous, I am going to claim partial credit. And a portion of his paycheck.

## 29  EDITORS WITH NO MERCY

Many years ago, I began writing a novel with the goal of publishing it one day. Once finished, I had the manuscript professionally edited, which was a painful experience. I submitted a manuscript that was black and white, and it came back covered in red. On every line. Rather humbling. But it was a necessary process and the changes have made for a much stronger piece of writing.

Then I had a great idea. We could read my manuscript aloud and count it as one of our hundred books. It seemed like a great way to test my material on the target audience and gain feedback.

Any visions I had of sweet support and enthusiastic cheering quickly faded. My kids were brutal! Nothing escaped their keen ears. They found things the professional editor had missed – with a candy reward for each correction, of course. I was seriously impressed with their editorial skills. Not only did they catch grammatical mistakes, but they also identified inconsistencies in characters and the plot as well as other minor flaws.

It wasn't all bad. They were encouraging in their comments. But it seemed more fun to find the mistakes. I'd like to think it's because they wanted to help make my manuscript the best it could be. But I know they also enjoyed the opportunity to correct their mom.

It took eighteen years from start to finish, but I am happy to announce that *Girls, Guys and a Tangle of Ties* is available on Amazon.com.

I believe that I wrote a good book. Maybe even a great one. But it is even better because of the sharp skills of my kids.

# 30 AT WAR WITH TECHNOLOGY

When we started reading, my children didn't have phones. They didn't have laptop computers. It was easy to limit television and gaming time. We could turn off these devices.

In my opinion, those were happier times. Things changed quickly once my kids got personal devices. And not for the better.

I admit there are many benefits to modern technology. But I have come to believe the list of drawbacks is longer, and the consequences more serious for our young people and society.

I will exercise self-control and not launch on a personal rant against the evils of technology and how our kids are becoming increasingly isolated, lack real-life interaction and relational skills, crave validation from media likes, are exposed to dangerous and addicting sexual content...No, I will control myself and resist the urge to shout about the dangers of digital devices.

But the truth is that I'm in a war with technology. Much is at stake. I am fighting for the time and attention of my children.

Reading has been one of my best weapons to counter devices. We've found that a combination approach works best. Set a time limit on devices. Then set a time for daily reading. More time on devices can be earned by more time reading.

I would be remiss if I didn't put in a plug for paper books. While I understand the convenience of digital devices, I choose to read printed paper books and have insisted on the same for my kids.

Studies have shown the benefits of holding and reading a tangible, page-turning book. Studying is more effective, and information is better retained when handling a real book. Even though schools offer access to online textbooks, I required my kids to sign out a heavy tome and lug it home from school.

I am sure my kids will thank me one day, both for the heavy textbooks and for limiting their time on technology. Currently, I am still waiting for expressions of their gratitude. Good thing I'm patient.

# 31  ONCE UPON A COLLEGE ESSAY

I recently had the privilege of editing multiple college application essays for the high school seniors of several friends. We've known each other as far back as kindergarten.

The college application essay is an unusual beast.

In most middle and high school classes, essays are based on an analytical and/or research format. However, college entrance essays are different. They require narrative writing with a strong sales pitch. Many students have not had a lot of practice with this personal style. Yet the college essay is one of the most important aspects of the application.

As I worked with each essay, I read them through several times. The first pass was to find basic grammatical mistakes. But then the remainder of my time and effort focused on structure and style.

For every essay that I read, the basic message has been the same. Create a better story. Draw a better picture. The reader should see you, hear you and smell you! Emphasize the weight of your challenges at the beginning. Describe the pain as you wipe the sweat from your brow. At the conclusion, the reader should rejoice with your victory.

It's a personal story. Tell it with passion and personality.

One of the benefits of reading is that my kids have absorbed hundreds of stories. Now it's their turn to go forth and tell their own.

# 32  COLLEGE TEST SCORES

My kids recently took the ACT test.

When I drove my son to take the 3-hour the exam, I fumed the entire way. He hadn't prepared at all, and I was not pleased. Many students choose some form of preparation, whether it's an online tutorial or a formal class. Some families invest a large amount of time and money.

My son did nothing to prepare. To his joy and my relief, he did extremely well on the test. His highest score was in the Science section, but only lower by one point were the Reading and English sections.

My daughter did some prep work on her own, took the test and also achieved an excellent score. Her strongest academic skill area? The Reading section was by far the highest, and the English section was second highest.

My kids would tell you that the test was easy and there was no need to study too much.

But I would tell you that our reading paid off.

## 33  COLLEGE COMFORT

My kids didn't call too much when they were away at college, but when they did, they often needed something. Sometimes it was advice or counsel. More times it was money. But sometimes they simply needed comfort.

My daughter called me on two separate occasions needing comfort. The first time, she suffered from a terrible migraine. The second time, she battled a terrible case of food poisoning.

There wasn't much I could do. It was late at night. We were hours of driving apart. I tried to give advice, suggested a few things that might help, and then was at a loss.

On both occasions, my daughter didn't want to be alone. She asked if I would stay with her on the phone and read to her.

That's exactly what I did. I pulled out one of her favorite books and proceeded to read. I read for hours, pausing only when she needed to vomit in the toilet. Finally, in a tired voice, my daughter said the worst had passed and she thought she could finally fall asleep. She said good night and we ended our call.

I can't express the frustration of being so far away and feeling so helpless. But I also can't express the relief at being able to do something to help ease my daughter's pain. Listening as I read a favorite story brought distraction from her physical suffering. It helped pass the hours of painful purging. It provided a familiar comfort during a difficult time.

I am so glad that we had the habit of reading to fall back on in her time of need.

## 34  COME FURTHER UP, COME FARTHER IN!

We've walked this adventure of reading together for over ten years. I know that a day is coming, sooner than I would like, when my children will no longer be living at home. Our journey of reading aloud as a family will come to an end. In fact, I have a feeling that we may be reading our last book even as I write this. Our copy of Atlas Shrugged has 1168 pages, and we're only on page 321, so it may take us months to finish. But even if this is not quite the end, someday there will be a last book.

I'd like to think that it's not really the end but simply time for my kids to set off on their own adventures.

I hope Nicholas and GrAce will continue to read for the rest of their lives. Currently, my daughter is reading more than my son. He would argue that he's busy with school, work, a few hobbies and multiple side projects. I know that I've put the habit of reading in him, and I have faith that as he finds more balance in his life, he'll be drawn back to books.

I hope Nicholas and GrAce will one day read to their children. Will this happen? I don't know. I can't see that far down the road. But if they don't, then I will!

All I know is that I've played my part. I've led the family on a Journey of Reading. We've crossed deserts, forded rivers, explored jungles, and gone farther than I ever could have imagined. It's everything I hoped for and so much more. We've climbed a mountain 142 books high.

But it's not the end. It's just a great place to point out other mountains that my children will scale on their own or with their families. As long as there are books to be read, there are adventures waiting to be taken.

We started our journey with the Chronicles of Narnia, and it seems only fitting to end with a quote from the last book in the series. In the *Last Battle*, the characters rush in wonder into the New Narnia. As they discover new delights and meet old friends, the cry of the unicorn, Jewel, is, "Come further up, come farther in!"

That is my cry as well. Tuck a good book under your arm and grab the hands of each person in your family.

Come further up, come farther in!

# ABOUT THE AUTHOR

Working with teenagers has been a passion for Galynne Matichuk, and she has over four decades of experience with young people in a variety of settings.

Galynne has nineteen years of middle and high school teaching experience in public schools in Canada and a private Christian school in the United States. She spent twelve summers working at summer camps, during which time she was a counselor, canoeing instructor, and camp speaker. For two years, Galynne worked with Teen Time, an inner-city teen ministry.

Galynne has enjoyed speaking at several camps, churches and had the privilege of leading several seminars at the California conference for the Association of Christian Schools International (ACSI) in California.

Galynne recently began working with the T.R.A.C. program (Teen Reach Adventure Camp, specifically designed for youth ages 12-15 in foster care) as a counsellor and camp speaker.

Galynne currently lives in Aledo, TX with her husband, near her two children, and with a ridiculous number of stuffed animals. The killer whale is especially badly behaved.

Galynne has one previous self-published novel entitled: *Girls, Guys, and a Tangle of Ties.*

www.ingramcontent.com/pod-product-compliance
Lightning Source LLC
Chambersburg PA
CBHW020554030426
42337CB00013B/1096